HARD AS NAILS IN

Ancient Rome

TRACEY TURNER

ILLUSTRATED BY JAMIE LENMAN

Crabtree Publishing Company
www.crabtreebooks.com

Crabtree Publishing Company
www.crabtreebooks.com
1-800-387-7650

616 Welland Ave.
St. Catharines, ON
L2M 5V6

PMB 59051, 350 Fifth Ave.
59th Floor,
New York, NY

Published by Crabtree Publishing Company in 2015.

Author: Tracey Turner

Illustrator: Jamie Lenman

Project coordinator: Kelly Spence

Editor: Becca Sjonger

Proofreader: Robin Johnson

Prepress technician: Samara Parent

Print coordinator: Margaret Amy Salter

Copyright © 2014 A & C Black

Text copyright © 2014 Tracey Turner

Illustrations copyright © 2014 Jamie Lenman

Additional illustrations © Shutterstock

First published 2014 by
A & C Black, an imprint of
Bloomsbury Publishing Plc.

Printed in Canada/022015/MA20150101

**Library and Archives Canada
Cataloguing in Publication**

Turner, Tracey, author
    Hard as nails in ancient Rome / Tracey Turner ; illustrated by Jamie Lenman.

(Hard as nails in history)
Includes index.
ISBN 978-0-7787-1513-9 (bound).--
ISBN 978-0-7787-1516-0 (pbk.)

    1. Rome--Biography--Juvenile literature.
2. Rome--History--
Juvenile literature. I. Lenman, Jamie, illustrator II. Title.

DG203.T87 2015   j937   C2014-908091-3

**Library of Congress
Cataloging-in-Publication Data**

Turner, Tracey.
 Hard as nails in ancient Rome / Tracey Turner ; illustrated by Jamie Lenman.
    pages cm. -- (Hard as nails in history)
 Includes index.
 ISBN 978-0-7787-1513-9 (reinforced library binding : alk. paper) --
ISBN 978-0-7787-1516-0 (pbk. : alk. paper)
 1. Rome--Biography--Juvenile literature. I. Lenman, Jamie, illustrator. II. Title.

 DG203.T87 2015
 937.009'9--dc23

2014046717

CONTENTS

INTRODUCTION	6
HANNIBAL	8
JOINING THE ROMAN ARMY	10
JULIUS CAESAR	12
AUGUSTUS CAESAR	14
BOUDICA	16
SPARTACUS	18
THERE'S NO PLACE LIKE ROME	20
VERCINGETORIX	22

EMPEROR NERO 24

SCIPIO THE GREAT 26

THE RISE AND FALL OF THE ROMAN EMPIRE 28

SULLA 30

FLAVIUS AETIUS 32

AGRIPPINA 34

GUIDE TO THE GODS 36

MARK ANTONY 38

TARQUIN THE PROUD 40

POMPEY THE GREAT 42

THE ROMAN EMPIRE GAME   44

CARACTACUS   46

EMPEROR TRAJAN   48

GALEN   50

ZENOBIA   52

FLAVIUS BELISARIUS   54

EMPEROR HADRIAN   56

HARD AS NAILS IN ANCIENT ROME TIMELINE   58

LEARNING MORE   61

GLOSSARY   62

INDEX   64

INTRODUCTION

This book describes the toughest men and women in ancient Roman history—or at least a selection of them, because there were a lot! Some were brave, some were clever, some were fearsome fighters, and some were absolutely awful. But they all were as hard as nails.

FIND OUT ABOUT . . .

• Marauding barbarians

• Barrels of snakes

• A conquering warrior queen

• Poisoners, assassins, and an emperor who killed his own mother

If you've ever wanted to enter the murderous world of Roman politics, join the Roman army, or conquer Mesopotamia, read on. Journey to the uncivilized frontiers of the empire, besieged cities in Gaul, and across the Alps by elephant.

As well as discovering stories of courage and cunning, you might be in for a few surprises. Did you know, for example, that Emperor Caligula's sister plotted to kill him? Or that Emperor Claudius's wife was a murderer?

Get ready to meet some of the toughest people in the history of ancient Rome . . .

Plus play the game on page 44 and see if you would have been tough enough to fight, persuade, conquer, and murder your way to the top of the Roman Empire!

HANNIBAL

Hannibal was a brilliant and ruthless North African general on a mission to stop the mighty Roman Empire in its tracks.

HARD AS NAILS RATING: 7.8

WAR WITH ROME

Hannibal was born in 247 BCE in Carthage, a city-state in North Africa. He was the son of general Hamilcar Barca. Carthage had its own empire, but the Romans thought Rome should be the only one doing any conquering. Carthage and Rome ended up fighting each other for 20 years, in what became known as the First Punic War. In the end, Carthage offered Rome the island of Sicily in exchange for peace. Rome accepted, but took Corsica and Sardinia as well—without them being offered!

SPANISH CONQUESTS

Hamilcar Barca, Hannibal's father, took revenge on Rome by conquering land in Spain. He took Hannibal with him. After his father died, Hannibal took over as general. By that time, he was 26 and already had some brilliant military ideas. He'd won a battle by tipping barrels of live snakes onto the deck of an enemy ship. He also planned to conquer the whole of Spain, and was making good progress.

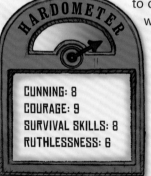

HARDOMETER

CUNNING: 8
COURAGE: 9
SURVIVAL SKILLS: 8
RUTHLESSNESS: 6

ELEPHANTS ACROSS THE ALPS

Rome was alarmed by Hannibal's progress in Spain and declared war on Carthage again. Hannibal decided to attack Rome in a way they'd never expect: from the north . . . with elephants!

He marched 90,000 foot soldiers, 12,000 horsemen, and 37 elephants from Spain, across the Pyrenees, through Gaul (now France and Belgium), over the Alps, and into Italy. The route—especially the mountains—was more difficult to travel than he'd thought, and the army was attacked by different enemies along the way. In the end, only 26,000 men and one elephant made it into Italy. Hannibal stayed there and battled the Romans for 15 years.

NO SURRENDER

Rome invaded Carthage and Hannibal was called back from Italy to help, but this time the Romans defeated him. Carthage agreed to peace terms. But Hannibal escaped and kept fighting the Romans. After many years, in about 183 BCE, the Romans finally cornered Hannibal and demanded his surrender. Instead, Hannibal chose death and poisoned himself.

JOINING THE ROMAN ARMY

The Romans didn't get their empire by asking nicely—they got it by sending in their army to kill anyone who stood in their way. Would you have been tough enough to join?

JOINING UP

You'll need to be a male Roman citizen (sorry, no girls), healthy, between the ages of 17 and 46, and you'll need to like marching long distances and fighting. You'll be well paid, well trained, and you won't go hungry. There are a few downsides, though: you have to sign up for 25 years, agree not to marry, and be willing to fight and die for Rome.

CENTURIES, COHORTS, AND LEGIONS

The ruthless Roman army was the most powerful and best organized army of its time. It had a rigid structure. A lowly citizen like you would be a foot soldier called a legionary, because you're part of a legion. Legions were organized into groups:

80 legionaries = 1 century
(a century means 100—at first there were 100 legionaries in a century, but the number was reduced to 80)

6 centuries = 1 cohort

10 centuries = 1 prima cohors

9 cohorts + 1 prima cohors = 1 legion

That's 5,120 men in every legion. There were about 30 legions in the Roman army.

TOP RANKING

Everyone in the army knows his place and, as a legionary, yours is at the bottom. A centurion is in charge of your century, and a legate is in charge of your whole legion. At the top, each general has command of several legions. And in charge of them is the emperor himself.

LOADING UP

Roman soldiers had to carry:

• Weapons and armor, including a three-foot-long (1 m) javelin and a 22-pound (10 kg) shield

• A spade for digging ditches when making camp

• Food and cooking utensils

• A heavy leather tent

That's more than 66 pounds (30 kg) of stuff for each person!

ROME'S LITTLE HELPERS

Not a Roman citizen? Good news! You can still become an auxiliary, or helper, soldier. Auxiliaries have fewer rights, are paid less money, and are given less training than legionaries, who will probably look down on you. However, you still have to do the fighting and dying part. But when you retire (if you live that long), you'll become a Roman citizen.

JULIUS CAESAR

Julius Caesar was a ruthless Roman leader and a brilliant general, who did plenty of conquering before making himself fatally unpopular.

HARD AS NAILS RATING: 8.3

REPUBLICAN ROME

When Julius Caesar was born, there hadn't been a king of Rome for more than 400 years. Rome was ruled by two consuls, who were elected from the senate and ruled for a year. There were 300 senators, who looked after things like lawmaking and going to war, and there was also an assembly of ordinary citizens who elected the consuls. Caesar had to wait to become a senator because he was living in exile while his enemy, Sulla, was busy executing anyone he didn't like in Rome. He wisely kept his distance until Sulla died.

GOVERNING AND CONQUERING

By the time Julius Caesar was back in Rome, he was known as a ruthless man, because of how he had bravely handled a group of pirates. He landed a series of top political jobs, including governor of Spain, which gave him the chance to show off his conquering skills. He invaded Portugal, killed many people, and brought huge amounts of loot back to Rome. He was just the kind of leader the Romans liked, and he was soon elected consul.

HARDOMETER

CUNNING: 8
COURAGE: 9
SURVIVAL SKILLS: 7
RUTHLESSNESS: 9

THREE LEADERS

Julius Caesar decided that being consul wasn't enough power for him. With two hard as nails general friends, Pompey and Crassus, he took control of Rome. Then he began a conquering spree: after eight years of hard battling, Gaul was ruled by Rome.

ONE LEADER

Crassus was killed in battle, and Pompey and Caesar went to war over who should be in charge. Caesar came out on top. Back in Rome, Caesar was made dictator of the empire for a period of ten years. But this wasn't enough for power-hungry Caesar. He made himself dictator for life. To the Romans, this was too close to being a king. A group of 23 senators put a stop to Caesar's ambitions by stabbing him to death.

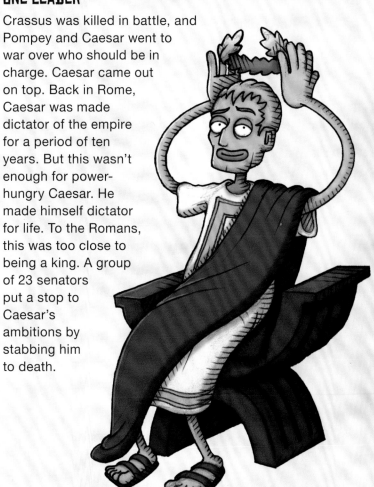

AUGUSTUS CAESAR

Augustus Caesar managed to do what Julius Caesar could not: he became the first emperor of Rome (though he was careful not to call himself that), and ruled the entire Roman world.

HARD AS NAILS RATING: 9

DEFEATING ENEMIES

Augustus was originally known as Octavian. He was born in Rome in 63 BCE, the great-nephew of Julius Caesar, who was assassinated when Octavian was 18. Julius Caesar named Octavian as his heir, and Octavian acted fast. In true ancient Roman style, Octavian raised an army and defeated Caesar's murderers, who were led by Brutus and Cassius. Octavian's friend Mark Antony helped him defeat his enemies. At first, they agreed to share power, together with another Roman leader, Lepidus. But it wasn't long before the plan changed. Octavian defeated Mark Antony at the Battle of Actium. Rome was now solely under Octavian's control.

DEFINITELY NOT A KING

Even though Octavian had all the power, he was careful not to say so or to look too much like a king, which had been Julius Caesar's big mistake. Octavian called himself "First Citizen," changed his name to Augustus, and reorganized the Roman army to make it more permanent. Doing so helped him stay in charge, and it also meant he could use the army to conquer more land.

HARDOMETER

CUNNING: 9
COURAGE: 9
SURVIVAL SKILLS: 9
RUTHLESSNESS: 9

EXPANDING TERRITORIES

Augustus wanted the empire to be a lot bigger. Under his control, the Roman army conquered Egypt, the rest of Spain, and chunks of central Europe. The German warriors proved too fierce even for the Romans, though. Thousands of men were lost and Germany managed to stay out of the Roman Empire.

AN IMPRESSIVE EMPIRE

By the time he died in 14 CE, Augustus had turned Rome from a republic ruled by elected politicians into an empire ruled by an emperor who inherited his title. Rome was now much bigger and richer. Many impressive new buildings were built, and the Roman army was stronger. Augustus paved the way for a long line of Roman emperors and an empire that would last (the eastern part, at least) for nearly 1,500 years.

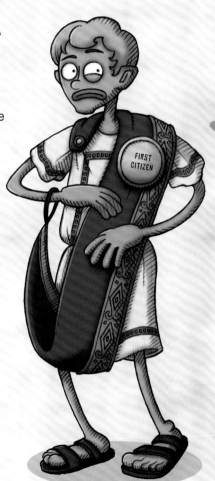

FIRST CITIZEN

BOUDICA

Boudica was a warrior queen in Roman Britain. She wasn't afraid to lead the Iceni people against the mighty Roman army.

HARD AS NAILS RATING: 7.5

RAMPAGING ROMANS

Boudica's husband, King Prasutagus of the Iceni, died in about 60 CE. The Romans thought that this was their opportunity to get their hands on the land in eastern England that belonged to the Iceni. They flogged Boudica, attacked her daughters, and stole property from the Iceni people. But they picked on the wrong woman.

REVOLTING BRITISH

Boudica raised an army of Iceni and other ancient Britons, and led them in a revolt against the Romans. She knew that the Roman army was already in charge of most of Britain, and they were well trained, armed to the teeth, and almost unstoppable. But she didn't care. She headed for the nearby Roman fort at Colchester, armed with war chariots, swords, and a burning sense of injustice.

AVENGING ARMY

Boudica and her army battered the Roman troops sent to fight them in Colchester. Then they turned toward London which, at the time, was a fairly small trading settlement. Suetonius, the Roman governor, was busy in Wales when he got news of Boudica's revolt. He marched to London right away.

HARDOMETER

CUNNING: 7
COURAGE: 9
SURVIVAL SKILLS: 7
RUTHLESSNESS: 7

But when he got there, he took one look at Boudica's angry army and led the Romans out of London instead of fighting.

BATTLING THE ROMANS

Boudica's troops smashed and burned as much of London as they could. Then they marched up to Saint Albans to the north, and smashed and burned that, too. Meanwhile, Suetonius gathered his forces. The two armies met in the middle of England. Boudica's army left their wagons and advanced toward the Romans, but they were met by a rain of Roman javelins. As the well-organized Roman troops approached, the Iceni army was pushed back, trapped by the line of wagons behind them.

FINAL DEFEAT

Boudica's brave army had finally met defeat. Thousands of British soldiers were killed. Boudica escaped the battlefield but, so the story goes, she took poison and killed herself rather than be captured by her hated Roman enemies.

SPARTACUS

Spartacus escaped from slavery and led a massive army of slave rebels who came close to defeating the powerful Roman army.

SPARTACUS THE SLAVE

Spartacus came from Thrace (modern-day Bulgaria), but no one knows much about his early life. He became a slave and was sent to a gladiator school near Capua in Italy, where he was trained to fight in gladiatorial games for the entertainment of bloodthirsty crowds. Sometimes this meant fighting to the death, so it's no wonder Spartacus wanted to escape.

ESCAPE FROM GLADIATOR SCHOOL

Spartacus plotted an escape in 73 BCE with around 200 other gladiators. But they were betrayed, and just as they were about to get away, the gladiator school guards leapt out to stop them. In the confusion, Spartacus and some of the others grabbed anything dangerous-looking they could find in the kitchens to use as weapons. About 70 of them managed to fight their way out.

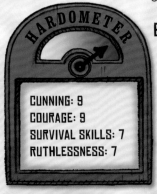

CUNNING: 9
COURAGE: 9
SURVIVAL SKILLS: 7
RUTHLESSNESS: 7

BASHING THE ROMANS

Spartacus and two other gladiators led the desperate band of runaways to Mount Vesuvius, recruiting more slaves along the way. Roman troops arrived to meet them and camped out, waiting for the rebels to appear. Meanwhile,

Spartacus and the slaves made ropes out of vines, rappelled down the mountain, took the Romans by surprise from behind, and defeated them. They went on to win more victories against the Romans. More and more rebellious slaves joined them until there were nearly 100,000 men ready to fight.

THE FINAL BATTLE

The slave army split into two groups. Spartacus led one, and the other was commanded by a slave called Crixus. It was completely slaughtered by the Romans—all 30,000 of them. Spartacus led his band of rebels north, fighting off Roman attacks on the way. By this time the Romans were worried: Spartacus seemed to be winning. They sent Crassus, one of their best generals, to stop him.

DEFEATED

Spartacus was finally defeated by Crassus in southern Italy in 71 BCE. Six thousand rebel slaves were crucified after the battle, and thousands more were killed by Roman troops. Spartacus's body was never found.

THERE'S NO PLACE LIKE ROME

Rome's empire was at its biggest in 117 CE, at the end of Emperor Trajan's reign and the start of Emperor Hadrian's. It stretched as far north as chilly Britain, and as far south as the sweltering deserts of North Africa. The area shaded in yellow on the map below shows the empire.

• The Romans first invaded Britain in 55 BCE, led by Julius Caesar, but only came to stay after Emperor Claudius's invasion in 43 CE.

- Rome conquered the whole of Italy by 265 BCE.

- The Romans were at war with Carthage for more than 100 years before finally conquering it in 146 BCE.

- The empire measured around 2,500 miles (4,000 km) from east to west in 117 CE.

- Emperor Hadrian decided the empire was too big, so he set fixed frontiers and even gave up some land in the Middle East.

Syria

- There were plenty of hostile groups at the edges of the empire. Roman forts were built along the frontiers to keep marauders at bay.

- People captured by the Romans were encouraged to live like the Romans, but they were allowed to worship their own gods and keep their own customs. They could become Roman citizens, and some of them joined the Roman army.

- The Romans often traded with barbarians, or people who lived outside the Roman Empire, and came to agreements with them so they didn't fight one another.

VERCINGETORIX

HARD AS NAILS RATING: 7.5

Vercingetorix was a hard as nails Gallic chieftain who stood up to the toughest and cleverest Roman general of them all: Julius Caesar.

CONQUERING GAUL

When Julius Caesar became governor of Transalpine Gaul (now southern France), the rest of Gaul wasn't under Roman control. Caesar wanted to conquer all of Gaul and had almost succeeded by 53 BCE. But that was when Vercingetorix, Gallic leader of the Arverni, got involved.

KING VERCINGETORIX

Vercingetorix's father had recently been executed by the Arverni for trying to make himself king. But that didn't stop Vercingetorix from trying the same thing himself. He raised an army, captured the Arverni capital, Gergovia, and was proclaimed king.

CAESAR MARCHES NORTH

Vercingetorix persuaded other Gallic groups to join forces against the Romans. Caesar marched his troops over mountains and through deep winter snow to arrive in the heart of Arverni territory. He was cold, irritable, and on the lookout for Vercingetorix.

HARDOMETER

CUNNING: 7
COURAGE: 8
SURVIVAL SKILLS: 7
RUTHLESSNESS: 8

RAMPAGING ROMANS AND GAULS

Caesar rampaged around the Arverni region, laying waste to one town after another and killing or enslaving everyone.

Vercingetorix rampaged in the opposite direction, burning all the towns behind him so that the Romans wouldn't have any food or shelter. In the spring of 52 BCE, Julius Caesar besieged Gergovia, but ended up losing many men there.

GAULS VS ROMANS

The Roman forces marched south. So did Vercingetorix's army of around 100,000—probably twice the number of Caesar's troops. But when the two sides met, the better trained and armed Romans won. Vercingetorix and his army ran away to the town of Alesia. The Romans surrounded and besieged the town, building massive fortifications to stop anyone from getting in or out. Despite his efforts to fight off the Romans and send messages for help, Vercingetorix was forced to surrender.

VERCINGETORIX'S END

Vercingetorix spent the next few years in prison in Rome. Caesar paraded him through the streets of Rome before finally executing him in 46 BCE.

EMPEROR NERO

Emperor Nero got to rule Rome only because of his mother, but he was so ruthless that he had her murdered, along with anyone else who stood in his way.

YOUNG EMPEROR

Nero became emperor when his uncle, Emperor Claudius, died in 54 CE. Nero's mother, Agrippina (see page 34), managed to get everyone else with a claim to the throne out of the way, and probably murdered Claudius, so that Nero could be emperor. At first, he ruled with Agrippina because he was only 16. But in less than two years, he managed to throw her out of the imperial palace. It's also likely that Nero had his stepbrother Britannicus poisoned, because he was Emperor Claudius's son.

MORE MURDERING

To stop Agrippina from interfering, Nero took drastic measures: after a couple of failed attempts involving boats and collapsing beds, he had her assassinated. His story was that Agrippina had sent an assassin to murder him in the imperial palace because he didn't want to rule alongside her.

HARDOMETER

CUNNING: 7
COURAGE: 8
SURVIVAL SKILLS: 6
RUTHLESSNESS: 10

PARTY TIME

With his mother out of the way, Nero concentrated on what he was good at: chariot racing, music, poetry, and partying. He divorced his wife, Octavia, had her executed, married his girlfriend Poppaea,

and embarked on expensive building projects and entertainment, which used large amounts of money raised by taxes. People started to get annoyed with Nero.

THE GREAT FIRE OF ROME

In 64 CE, fire spread through Rome. Nero didn't seem too concerned about it and so he became even less popular. Unwisely, he started building at the site of the fire. One of the grand buildings was the Golden House, a luxurious new palace for himself. To pay for it, he took treasure from temples around the empire, which caused a rebellion in Jerusalem.

THE LAST STRAW

While Nero was on a tour of Greece, everyone turned on him. The senate condemned him to be flogged to death in 69 CE. Rather than face his grisly sentence, Nero fled. It's thought that he took his own life by cutting his throat.

SCIPIO THE GREAT

**HARD AS NAILS
RATING: 8·8**

**Scipio was a fearsome
Roman general who finally
defeated Hannibal of Carthage,
and ended the Second Punic War.**

DEFEAT BY ROME

Scipio came from a long line of warlike Scipios. His
grandfather and father did their fair share of fighting in the
war with Carthage, the tough North African empire that
Rome was determined to conquer. At the Battle of Ticinus,
18-year-old Scipio saved his father's life. But things were
not going well for the Romans: they lost the battle, and they
went on to even worse defeats at the hands of Carthaginian
general Hannibal (see page 8). In 211 BCE, Scipio's father
and uncle were both killed in battle with the Carthaginians
in Spain.

SCIPIO IN SPAIN

No one else in Rome dared to lead the Roman army in
Spain against the ferocious Carthaginians. But Scipio was
tough enough to take the job. Once he was given command
of his own troops, he never lost a battle.

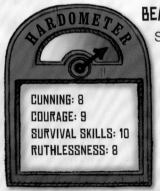

CUNNING: 8
COURAGE: 9
SURVIVAL SKILLS: 10
RUTHLESSNESS: 8

BEATING THE CARTHAGINIANS

Scipio battered the Carthaginians
at Ilipa in the south of Spain in
206 BCE. By the end of the year,
his army had managed to push
the Carthaginians out of Spain
completely. In 205 BCE, he was
made consul, and he persuaded
Rome to invade North Africa
while Hannibal was busy

rampaging around Italy, causing as much damage as he could.

AFRICAN VICTORY

Hannibal returned from Italy in 202 BCE to fight Scipio near Carthage at the Battle of Zama. Despite Hannibal's 80 war elephants, Scipio won. He conquered the northern part of Africa, and ended the Second Punic War with Carthage. He returned to Rome in triumph and was given an extra name after his conquest: Africanus.

RETIRING FROM ROME

Scipio Africanus and his brother, Scipio Asiaticus, led another Roman victory, this time in Syria. Despite his victories, Scipio didn't stay in favor in Rome, and went to live in the south of Italy. He died around 183 BCE, probably in the same year as his old enemy, Hannibal.

SCIPIO AFRICANUS

THE RISE AND FALL OF THE ROMAN EMPIRE

It took hundreds of years for the city of Rome to grow into a great empire, and another few hundred years for it to get battered down to size by barbarians.

ROMULUS AND REMUS

Amost 3,000 years ago, people settled on the hilltops above the Tiber, a river in Italy. Their villages gradually grew into the city of Rome. But in Roman legend, two twins, Romulus and Remus, were abandoned by their parents. They were saved and raised by a female wolf. After a terrible fight, Romulus killed Remus and went on to found the city of Rome, named after himself.

KICKING OUT THE KINGS

Rome was ruled by kings, until the Roman people became angry with them and kicked them out. The last king was Tarquin the Proud, whose reign ended in 509 BCE. Rome became a republic, ruled by elected politicians headed by two consuls.

COUNTRY CONQUERING

By around 265 BCE, the Romans had conquered the rest of Italy and started on other countries. Some of them put up a fight, but eventually Rome controlled most of the land around the Mediterranean Sea.

GENERALS AND EMPERORS

After 500 years as a republic, things began to change in Rome. Julius Caesar became almost like a king, until he was stabbed to death. It wasn't long before the end of the Roman Republic and the start of the Roman Empire. The first emperor was Augustus Caesar, Julius Caesar's heir.

AN ENORMOUS EMPIRE

There was already a big empire waiting for the first Roman emperor. After more conquering, it kept growing until, in the reign of the thirteenth emperor, Trajan, it reached the biggest it would ever be.

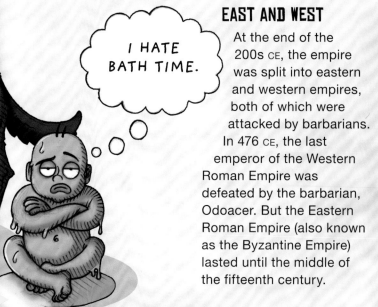

I HATE BATH TIME.

EAST AND WEST

At the end of the 200s CE, the empire was split into eastern and western empires, both of which were attacked by barbarians. In 476 CE, the last emperor of the Western Roman Empire was defeated by the barbarian, Odoacer. But the Eastern Roman Empire (also known as the Byzantine Empire) lasted until the middle of the fifteenth century.

SULLA

Sulla was one of Rome's toughest and most ruthless leaders. He was most famous for his brutal executions.

OUTSMARTIN' THE NUMIDIANS

Sulla's first big victory was in North Africa, against King Jugurtha of Numidia. Jugurtha had successfully battered the Roman army in 111 and 110 BCE. Sulla ended the conflict by persuading another African king to betray and kidnap Jugurtha for the Romans. But Marius, who commanded the campaign, got the credit for the Roman victory. This started a rivalry between Sulla and Marius that would become a major clash.

MARCHING ON ROME

Sulla gained a reputation as a tough guy. In 87 BCE he was sent to deal with King Mithridates of Pontus, who was causing problems for Rome in the area that's now northwestern Turkey. Marius was angry: *he* had wanted the chance to defeat King Mithridates and get the glory. So he persuaded the senate to call Sulla back. Sulla was absolutely furious. So furious that he marched on Rome at the head of six legions. This meant civil war! He lost no time in taking control of the city. Then Sulla dusted himself off and went back to Pontus to finish his business with King Mithridates.

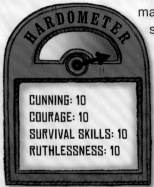

HARDOMETER

CUNNING: 10
COURAGE: 10
SURVIVAL SKILLS: 10
RUTHLESSNESS: 10

DICTATOR OF ROME

Meanwhile, with Sulla away, Marius led his own march on Rome to try and capture the city himself. He caused a lot of death and destruction, and even outlawed Sulla. But Marius died the following year. Sulla, even more angry by this time, marched on Rome again. Helped by the generals Crassus and Pompey (see page 42), he ended the Roman civil war once and for all. Sulla was now dictator of Rome.

SULLA'S EXECUTIONS

Sulla began a reign of terror. He drew up lists of his enemies, which were called proscriptions. They included anyone he thought couldn't be counted on to support him. Then he had them executed. He was accused of proscribing rich people just so he could steal their possessions. In the end, thousands of people were killed because of Sulla's proscriptions. Perhaps worn out with all that executing, Sulla stepped down from office in 79 BCE, and died the following year.

PROSCRIPTIONS

FLAVIUS AETIUS

HARD AS NAILS RATING: 8.5

Flavius Aetius was a barbarian-bashing general who led the Roman army in the last desperate years of the Western Roman Empire.

MARAUDING BARBARIANS

By the 400s CE, the Roman Empire had divided into two. Things were not going well, especially in the western empire, and barbarians made constant attacks. When the Romans weren't defending themselves, they were making pacts with the barbarians to keep them quiet. From 405 to 408 CE, when Flavius Aetius was a child, he was sent as a hostage to Alaric I, the king of the Visigoths. Noble Roman hostages such as Aetius were like a promise that the Romans would keep their side of an agreement. Then, in a similar arrangement, Aetius went to stay with the Huns. He ended up living and fighting alongside them for years.

VALENTINIAN, VISIGOTHS, AND FRANKS

Aetius was made commander of the Roman army in Gaul, which was just the kind of job he liked, since it gave him the perfect opportunity to batter barbarians. First he drove back the Visigoths, then he defeated the Franks . . . then the Visigoths again, and then the Franks again. Meanwhile, Aetius was worried that another hard as nails general, Bonifacius, might be doing better than he was—so he marched against him and defeated him. Aetius was now

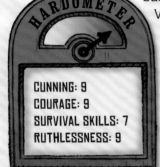

HARDOMETER

CUNNING: 9
COURAGE: 9
SURVIVAL SKILLS: 7
RUTHLESSNESS: 9

the most powerful general and politician in the Western Roman Empire. However, Valentinian III, a young boy whose mother ruled as regent, was the emperor.

ATTILA ATTACKS

The next few years saw plenty more barbarian bashing. Attila was the leader of Aetius's old friends the Huns. Attila was on good terms with Aetius, but eventually the Hun couldn't resist it any longer: he attacked Gaul. Aetius persuaded the Visigoths to join him against the Huns and, in 451 CE, the Romans and Visigoths defeated them. The following year Attila was back, rampaging around Italy, until eventually he was chased away by Aetius's army.

VALENTINIAN GETS VIOLENT

Aetius didn't die in battle. Valentinian grew up to be suspicious of him: he thought Aetius wanted his own son to be emperor. In 454 CE, Valentinian leapt at Aetius with a sword, accusing him of treason, and killed him. Six months later, Valentinian was killed by a Hun assassin.

AGRIPPINA

Agrippina rose to be the most powerful woman in Rome, and she got there by plotting, scheming, and probably poisoning.

THE EMPEROR'S SISTER

Agrippina the Younger was the great-granddaughter of the first Roman emperor, Augustus Caesar. When she was 21, her brother Caligula became emperor. He gave Agrippina and her two sisters, Drusilla and Livilla, special privileges. However, when Drusilla died of a sudden illness, Caligula stopped being so nice to the other two. Instead, he started behaving very strangely: he demanded to be worshiped as a god, made his horse a priest, and ordered his army to collect seashells.

PLOT OF THE THREE DAGGERS

Agrippina didn't like the way things were turning out. She, her sister, and their cousin Lepidus plotted to murder Caligula and make Lepidus emperor. But the "Plot of the Three Daggers" was discovered. Lepidus was executed and the two sisters were exiled.

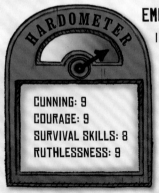

HARDOMETER

CUNNING: 9
COURAGE: 9
SURVIVAL SKILLS: 8
RUTHLESSNESS: 9

EMPEROR UNCLE CLAUDIUS

In 41 CE, Caligula was murdered by his own bodyguard. Claudius, Agrippina's uncle, became emperor, and he called the sisters back to Rome. Agrippina married a rich and powerful man, who died a few years later. The rumor was that she'd poisoned her husband to get his money.

EMPRESS OF ROME

Emperor Claudius's wife, Messalina, was executed in 48 CE for plotting to kill him. Even though she was his niece, Agrippina married Claudius the next year. She became the most powerful woman in Rome—the empress. She persuaded Claudius to adopt Nero, her son by her first marriage, as his heir instead of his own three children.

MORE MURDERING

The story goes that Agrippina killed Claudius with poisonous mushrooms when he began to regret marrying her. This meant her son Nero became emperor of Rome. But he didn't thank his mother for putting him there. Nero threw Agrippina out of the imperial palace as quickly as he could.

EVEN MORE MURDERING

There's a story that Agrippina swam to shore after Nero sank a boat she was traveling on, and that she survived another murder attempt by her son when he rigged a bed to collapse on top of her. Finally, Nero sent assassins to kill her, and Agrippina died in 59 CE.

YOU LIKE MUSHROOMS, DON'T YOU DARLING?

GUIDE TO THE GODS

The Romans worshiped many gods and goddesses—about 20 main ones, mostly borrowed from the ancient Greeks but given Roman names. For example, Zeus, the Greek king of the gods, was the Roman god Jupiter; the Greek goddess of love, Aphrodite, was the Roman goddess Venus; and Ares, the Greek god of war, was the Roman god Mars.

A GOD FOR EVERYTHING

There were also household gods who protected the home, gods of food storage, and even a god of a type of mold that attacks wheat—there was an annual festival to please him so that the corn would be spared. Abstract qualities, like "discipline" and "youth," were worshiped as gods, too. Some emperors, including Augustus, Trajan, Hadrian, and Claudius, had themselves made into gods after they died.

TRUE OR FALSE?

How many of these goddesses do you think are real, and how many are made up?

- Cloacina, goddess of sewers
- Annona, goddess of the grain supply to the city of Rome
- Cardea, goddess of door hinges
- Bubona, goddess of cattle
- Iris, goddess of the rainbow
- Mellona, goddess of bees
- Nemesis, goddess of revenge
- Deverra, goddess of brooms used to purify temples

FOUL FESTIVALS

In honor of all those gods, the Romans celebrated many festivals. They often included animal sacrifices to please the gods. A "haruspex" was a Roman priest who made predictions about the future by looking at the splattered guts of sacrificed animals.

EVEN MORE GODS

The Romans were happy to add foreign gods of countries they'd conquered to their huge collection. At least this meant one less thing to argue about with the natives. Near Hadrian's Wall, for example, the Romans set up a shrine to Brigantia, goddess of a northern British group. Mithraism was a Persian religion that became popular with the Roman army. Eventually, with Constantine the Great, the Romans adopted Christianity as their main religion.

Answer: They're all real Roman goddesses.

MARK ANTONY

A tough Roman army commander and persuasive politician, Mark Antony became one of the most powerful men in the world, before losing everything to Augustus Caesar.

CONQUERING GAUL AND GOVERNING ITALY

Mark Antony charged into history by leading horsemen in Judea and Egypt. He later fought alongside his distant relative, Julius Caesar (see page 12), in his conquest of Gaul. He governed Italy while Caesar was off conquering, and he fought with Caesar in his victory over Pompey (see page 43) at the Battle of Pharsalus.

OVER CAESAR'S DEAD BODY

Caesar tried to make himself dictator for life, which upset some senators so much that they stabbed him to death in 44 BCE. Mark Antony gave a rousing speech at Caesar's funeral, pointing out his stab wounds and naming the senators who had made each one.

THREE'S A CROWD

Mark Antony formed a three-man alliance, called a "triumvirate," with Marcus Aemilius Lepidus and Caesar's heir, Octavian. They took control of Rome. When the senate tried to kick them out, they had 130 senators murdered. The triumvirate also had to deal with two of Caesar's old enemies, Cassius and Brutus, and defeated them in

HARDOMETER

CUNNING: 8
COURAGE: 9
SURVIVAL SKILLS: 7
RUTHLESSNESS: 8

battle in 42 BCE. Octavian returned to Rome, Mark Antony looked after Roman territory in the east, and Lepidus took control of Spain and North Africa.

TROUBLESOME WOMEN

When Mark Antony's wife Fulvia had an argument with Octavian, she didn't just shout and storm off: she raised eight legions and fought a battle against him. Octavian won, though, and Mark Antony divorced Fulvia and married Octavia, Octavian's sister. But then he upset everyone by going to Egypt and falling in love with Cleopatra.

BATTLE OF ACTIUM

Octavian was angry with Mark Antony, and he forced Lepidus to resign. Cleopatra claimed that her and Julius Caesar's son, Caesarion, was the true heir to the Roman Empire, and Mark Antony supported her, so they went to war with Octavian. At the Battle of Actium, Octavian won and Mark Antony killed himself. Rather than be brought as a prisoner to Rome, Cleopatra killed herself, too.

TARQUIN THE PROUD

Tarquin was a ruthless, murderous, greedy tyrant. No wonder he was the last king of Rome.

HARD AS NAILS RATING: 8.3

LEGENDARY KINGS

According to Roman tradition, the first king of Rome was Romulus, who'd been reared by a she-wolf before he founded Rome. Some of what we know about Tarquin the Proud might be legendary, too. He was the seventh king of Rome, who ruled from 534 to 509 BCE.

MURDER IN THE FAMILY

Tarquin was either the son or grandson of the fifth king of Rome, but he was passed over in favor of Servius Tullius. Servius Tullius gave his two daughters to be married to Tarquin and his brother. However, Tarquin and his brother's wife, Tullia, preferred each other to their own mates, so they had Tarquin's brother and Tullia's sister murdered, then got married. After, Tarquin had Servius Tullius murdered so that he could take his place as king. The story goes that Tullia then ran over the dead body of Servius Tullius—her own father—with her chariot.

HARDOMETER

CUNNING: 8
COURAGE: 7
SURVIVAL SKILLS: 9
RUTHLESSNESS: 9

TERRIBLE TIMES

Tarquin began his reign by murdering any senators he suspected of supporting the previous king. This reduced the size of the senate, and he ruled as a dictator. He conquered towns surrounding Rome and took their wealth, which the Romans probably wouldn't have minded, but they did mind that he hadn't asked them first. Eventually, a group of senators rebelled against Tarquin and kicked him out in 509 BCE.

REPUBLICAN ROME

The Roman Republic, with elected leaders called consuls, began after Tarquin's exile. He sent his sons to start a conspiracy, but it didn't work and the sons were executed. Next, Tarquin stirred up trouble with Rome's neighboring cities, and he led attacks on Rome. He was defeated at the Battle of Silva Arsia, but he didn't give up. He persuaded Lars Porsena of Clusium to attack Rome—and this time the Romans were beaten. They still wouldn't let Tarquin return home, though.

FINAL DEFEAT

Tarquin turned to his son-in-law, who ruled a group of Latin villages near Rome, for help. When Rome beat the Latins, Tarquin finally admitted defeat. He went to stay with the Greek tyrant, Aristodemus of Cumae. Tarquin died the following year, in 495 BCE.

POMPEY THE GREAT

HARD AS NAILS RATING: 8.8

Pompey was a great general and politician, but Julius Caesar was his downfall.

TAKING SIDES

Pompey was born in Rome in 106 BCE. He lost no time in showing he was a rough, tough, conquering Roman. He sided with the ruthless general Sulla (see page 30) in Sulla's civil war against Marius, and led victories for him in Africa and Sicily. He harshly executed Marius's generals if they surrendered, and earned the nickname "Sulla's butcher" from his enemies.

TRIUMPH, CONQUERING, AND CRUSHING

Pompey was given a "triumph," or parade through the city of Rome to celebrate his victory, which gave him a chance to show off. When Sulla stepped down from being dictator of Rome, Pompey went to Spain to fight against one of Marius's generals, and reconquered Spain. By then he was very powerful. He returned to Italy in time to help crush Spartacus's rebellion (see page 18). Pompey was made consul in 70 BCE, together with his rival Crassus.

POMPEY'S PIRATES

HARDOMETER

CUNNING: 9
COURAGE: 9
SURVIVAL SKILLS: 8
RUTHLESSNESS: 9

Pirates were a menace in the Mediterranean Sea, and Pompey was the obvious choice to solve the problem. He took control of the Mediterranean for Rome with little trouble, and helped resettle the pirates so that they wouldn't come back. Then Pompey was off to fight King Mithridates in Pontus. He also made an alliance with the Armenians, captured Jerusalem, and made Syria a Roman province. Phew!

POMPEY, CRASSUS, AND CAESAR

In 59 BCE, Pompey joined Crassus and Caesar to form a three-man alliance, and he married Julia, Julius Caesar's daughter. But by 54 BCE, Julia had died, and Crassus had been killed in battle. Pompey and Julius Caesar competed for power. Pompey persuaded the senators to back him instead of Caesar. The senate asked Caesar to give up his army. In reply, Caesar marched his army on Rome, declaring himself at war with Pompey.

LOSING HIS HEAD

Pompey met Julius Caesar at the Battle of Pharsalus. Although Caesar had a smaller army and his soldiers were tired, he managed to outwit Pompey and win the battle. Pompey was forced to run away to Egypt. But the Egyptian leader Ptolemy betrayed him: he killed Pompey, cut off his head, and offered it to Caesar as a gift.

I HAVE A LOT TO DO SO JUST BEHAVE YOURSELF!

THE ROMAN EMPIRE GAME

For two to six players. You'll need a game piece for each person and a dice to play this game.

BEGIN YOUR TRIP TO THE IMPERIAL PALACE HERE.

2

Get your first job in politics. Go forward three spaces.

Battered by barbarians in a surprise attack. Go back two spaces.

10

12

13

Win a victory over some rebellious Britons. Go forward two spaces.

15

16

24

23

Besieged by marauding Gauls. Miss a turn.

Assassinated by a political rival. Go back to the start.

Conquer new territory, enslave thousands, and celebrate a triumph in Rome. Roll again.

27

You're ambitious Roman citizens on the path to power in the Roman Empire. Which of you will be tough enough to fight, persuade, conquer, and murder your way to the top?

4

Pirates attack in the Mediterranean Sea. Go back three spaces.

6

Given command of the army in Gaul. Go forward three spaces.

EXILE

9

Forced into exile when your political opponent gets into power. Miss a turn.

Elected consul. Roll again.

18

Struck down by plague. Miss two turns.

21

Marry the emperor's daughter. Go forward four spaces.

Murder your main rival. Go forward two spaces.

29

The emperor dies and the army wants YOU to take his place.

HAIL CAESAR!

CARACTACUS

**HARD AS NAILS
RATING: 8.8**

British chieftain Caractacus was not happy about the Roman invasion, so he did something about it in the only way he knew how.

THE ROMANS ARRIVE

Caractacus was chieftain of the Catuvellauni in southeast England. The Romans invaded in 43 CE under Emperor Claudius, and then made agreements with British leaders who were happy to accept Roman rule.

FRIENDLY ROMANS

To many of the British chieftains, Roman rule seemed like a fair deal—they got the protection of the Roman army and they could keep their own religion and customs. Plus, the Romans wouldn't kill them. But Caractacus didn't agree with Roman rule. He began to attack Roman-friendly Britons, including King Verica of the Atrebates.

ROMANS VS BRITONS

King Verica fled to Rome and asked Emperor Claudius to help fight Caractacus. Claudius arrived in Britain with a force of 40,000 soldiers. They landed in Kent, where they faced an army of Britons, including Caractacus. The Romans won and most of the defeated Britons came to agreements with Claudius, and accepted the Romans.

HARDOMETER

CUNNING: 8
COURAGE: 9
SURVIVAL SKILLS: 10
RUTHLESSNESS: 8

CARACTACUS GOES WEST

But not Caractacus. He went westward until he found another group that was tough enough to join him—the Silures, from modern-day South Wales. The Romans had a better equipped and better trained army, but Caractacus had the advantage of knowing the country. In 50 CE, he gathered together an army of the Catuvellauni, the Silures, and anyone else he could persuade to stand up to the Romans.

WELSH DEFEAT

Caractacus gave a rousing speech, reminding his troops that their ancestors had already driven out one army of Romans, Julius Caesar's, more than 100 years before. The British forces met the Romans bravely and fiercely, but the Roman army was just too good for them. Caractacus tried to find refuge with Cartimandua, Queen of the Brigantes, but he was caught, put in chains, and handed over to the Romans.

HAPPY ENDING

Amazingly, rather than executing Caractacus, Claudius spared him and his family. They all had a happy retirement in southern Italy.

EMPEROR TRAJAN

Thanks to Trajan's relentless conquering, the Roman Empire grew to be the biggest it would ever be.

HARD AS NAILS RATING: 8.5

TRAJAN'S HERO

Trajan became emperor in 98 CE. His hero was Julius Caesar (see page 12), who was famous for winning new territory for Rome. Trajan lost no time in doing some conquering of his own.

EMPIRE BUILDING

Trajan was an experienced soldier. He was 45 by the time he became emperor, and he'd already commanded the Roman army in northwestern Spain, and ended a rebellion by the Roman governor of Germany. He started by bringing Arabia Petraea (now the Sinai peninsula, plus parts of Jordan and Saudi Arabia) under Roman control. Then he led his army against King Decebalus of Dacia (modern-day Romania), and successfully conquered the country, which happened to contain several gold mines. To celebrate, King Decebalus's head was put on display in Rome, and Trajan's Column was built—an almost 100-foot-tall (30 m) column sculpted with glorious highlights from the war with Dacia.

HARDOMETER

CUNNING: 8
COURAGE: 9
SURVIVAL SKILLS: 9
RUTHLESSNESS: 8

MORE CONQUERING

But Trajan wasn't finished. He went on to conquer Mesopotamia (modern-day Iraq) as well. Trajan also fought Mesopotamia's neighbor, Parthia (modern-day Iran) and conquered parts of that, too.

LOOT!

All that conquering meant that Rome collected slaves—half a million of them—and treasure. With the loot from the conquered lands, Trajan introduced help for poor children, reduced the amount people had to pay in taxes, and built new and impressive buildings in Rome. He also introduced a gruesome three-month-long festival in the Colosseum in Rome, in which chariot racing and fights with gladiators and wild animals provided blood-thirsty entertainment.

NO MORE CONQUERING

Trajan had done more conquering than any other Roman. But just before he had a chance to finish off the Parthians for good, he died suddenly in 117 CE. The Roman Empire was now at its biggest, and the Roman army consisted of 400,000 men.

GALEN

Galen is the only hard-as-nails ancient Roman who didn't kill people—at least, not on purpose. He was the most famous ancient Roman doctor ever.

HARD AS NAILS RATING: 7.5

WOUNDED GLADIATORS

As a young man, Galen studied medicine in Greece and Egypt before returning to Pergamum (in modern-day Turkey) where he was born. He became chief doctor at the local gladiator school, so he had plenty of wounds to practice on. He called the gladiators' wounds "windows into the body," and he healed them so successfully that only five gladiators died in the five years he was their doctor.

DOCTORS AND PATIENTS

In around 162 CE, Galen moved to Rome. The other Roman doctors didn't like his newfangled ideas and plotted against him. Galen was so worried that they might poison him that he left Rome. But Emperor Marcus Aurelius called him back to become the doctor of the imperial court. Galen was the emperor's doctor and he also treated the two emperors who followed.

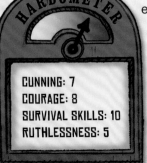

HARDOMETER

CUNNING: 7
COURAGE: 8
SURVIVAL SKILLS: 10
RUTHLESSNESS: 5

KIDNEYS, LUNGS, AND CATARACTS

When he wasn't treating emperors, Galen experimented: he dissected animals, inflated dead animals' lungs, and was especially interested in the spinal cords of pigs. He discovered that urine is formed inside kidneys (people thought it was formed in the bladder), found out what larynxes are for (so that we can speak), and that arteries carry blood. He was also a skilled surgeon, and performed delicate operations to remove cataracts from patients' eyes.

THE PLAGUE OF GALEN

One of the reasons Marcus Aurelius called Galen to Rome was an outbreak of plague, which swept through the Roman Empire. There were millions of deaths from the plague, with up to 2,000 people dying each day in Rome. Galen lived through the outbreak, treated its victims, and recorded its deadly progress. Today, the disease is thought to have been smallpox.

LASTING LEGACY

Galen lived until he was quite old— at least 70. His medical theories were still being used 1,500 years after his death.

I THINK YOU'LL LIVE. IT'S JUST A PAPER CUT.

ZENOBIA

Zenobia was a warrior queen. She revolted against the Romans, conquered Egypt, and built up her own empire.

QUEEN ZENOBIA

Around 258 CE, Zenobia married the king of Palmyra in Syria. Nine years later, the king and his son from a previous marriage were both assassinated, so Queen Zenobia ruled instead, with her one-year-old son, Vaballathus. Palmyra's neighbor was the Sassanid Empire, which was based in what's now Iran. It was rapidly expanding and causing trouble for the Romans in the process. Zenobia fought the Sassanids, saying that she was protecting the Roman Empire—though really she was winning new land for her own.

CONQUERING!

In 269 CE, Zenobia rode into battle with her army and conquered Egypt. She was helped by an Egyptian friend, Timagenes, and his army. She proclaimed herself queen of Egypt, and became known for her bravery, horse-riding skills, and as a warrior queen. But she didn't stop there: next Zenobia and the Palmyrenes conquered a big chunk of Anatolia (in modern-day Turkey), then Syria, Palestine, and Lebanon in the Middle East.

HARDOMETER

CUNNING: 9
COURAGE: 9
SURVIVAL SKILLS: 9
RUTHLESSNESS: 8

ZENOBIA VS THE ROMANS

The Romans, under Emperor Aurelian, had enough trouble from the Sassanids and their expanding empire, and they were furious to discover that Zenobia had started building her own empire as well. They came to meet her near Antioch (a city that's now in Turkey), and defeated the Palmyrene army.

ESCAPE AND CAPTURE

Zenobia escaped by camel, but she was soon captured by the Romans. Her Palmyrene Empire was defeated before it had a chance to get going. Any Palmyrenes who didn't surrender to the Romans were executed, and Zenobia and her son Vaballathus were taken to Rome. In 274 CE, Zenobia appeared in golden chains in Rome, so that everyone could see Emperor Aurelian's conquest.

ZENOBIA'S END

No one is sure what happened to Zenobia. There's a story that Aurelian was so impressed by Zenobia's bravery and beauty that he gave her a villa in Italy, where she married and lived a happy life.

FLAVIUS BELISARIUS

Flavius Belisarius was the greatest general of the Eastern Roman Empire, who reconquered huge chunks of the old Roman Empire.

HARD AS NAILS
RATING: 9

EASTERN COMMANDER

By the time Belisarius was born, the Western Roman Empire had already fallen to barbarians, and the Eastern Roman Empire, or Byzantine Empire, was ruled from Constantinople (modern-day Istanbul in Turkey). Belisarius joined the army under the Eastern Roman Emperor Justin I, and he did so well that the next emperor, Justinian I, gave him command of the whole army.

REBELLIONS, PERSIANS, AND VANDALS

In 532 CE, when Belisarius was 27, there was an uprising in Constantinople and he was sent to stop it. By the time Belisarius had dealt with it, around 30,000 people had been killed. He went on to win a series of awesome victories against the Persians. Then Belisarius lost no time in driving the Vandals out of Africa, making the African provinces Roman once again.

HARDOMETER

CUNNING: 9
COURAGE: 9
SURVIVAL SKILLS: 9
RUTHLESSNESS: 9

OSTROGOTHS IN ITALY

It was a busy few years for Belisarius. In 535 CE, he was sent to fight the Ostrogoths in Italy. Once he'd defeated them, the Ostrogoths wanted to make him their king. Belisarius pretended to go along with the idea, then had the Ostrogoth leaders arrested and claimed their empire for Emperor Justinian.

JEALOUS JUSTINIAN

Belisarius fought the Persians again, then he was back to Italy to crush a Goth rebellion in Rome. Belisarius captured the city, but Emperor Justinian called him back to Constantinople—he was worried that the handsome, charming general was too popular. Even after Belisarius fought back the invading Bulgars in 559 CE, Emperor Justinian wasn't happy. He accused Belisarius of made-up charges, and sent him to prison.

TOUGHEST EASTERN ROMAN

After all that conquering, rebellion-crushing, and invader-repelling, Belisarius was pardoned. He died three years later in 565 CE, at the age of 60, having won the admiration of just about everyone as the toughest man in the Eastern Roman Empire.

ARE YOU KIDDING ME?

EMPEROR HADRIAN

HARD AS NAILS RATING: 8.5

Hadrian inherited a vast empire. He fortified its frontiers, and made sure his army was powerful enough to hang on to it.

EXPANDED EMPIRE

Hadrian commanded troops in Emperor Trajan's battles, for which he was made governor of Syria. He became emperor of Rome when Trajan died. The first thing he did was have several senators killed, accusing them of conspiring against him. Because of Trajan's conquering, the empire had grown to a huge size. Hadrian decided it was too big, so he gave up Rome's new eastern territories in Mesopotamia.

TOUGH TROOPS

Hadrian wanted a tough, fit, well-trained, and well-disciplined army, so he spent as much time with the soldiers as he could, showing them that he could be just as tough as them. Hadrian traveled around his empire with his army, but rather than conquering, he concentrated on making its borders secure from marauders.

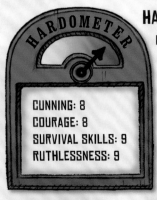

HARDOMETER

CUNNING: 8
COURAGE: 8
SURVIVAL SKILLS: 9
RUTHLESSNESS: 9

HADRIAN'S WALL

In 122 CE, Hadrian decided to take a trip somewhere cold, damp, and a stone's throw from hostile barbarians: Britain. He looked at the border of his empire, a road called the Stanegate that stretched across the north of Britain. Then he looked at what was on the other side: a bleak

landscape full of angry-looking people. So he ordered
a huge stone wall to be built—one that would keep the
barbarians where they belonged—called Hadrian's Wall.

WAR ON JERUSALEM

Hadrian waged one war while he was emperor, and he did
it with utter ruthlessness. In 130 CE, he visited the ruins
of Jerusalem (there had been a Roman-Jewish war that
ended in 73 CE) and rebuilt the city. But his anti-Jewish laws
sparked a revolt, and a fierce war raged for three years.
After the war, Hadrian sold many thousands of captured
Jews into slavery, and continued to make anti-Jewish
laws. Three years later, in 138 CE, Hadrian died, leaving his
slightly reduced empire to his heir, Antoninus Pius.

HARD AS NAILS IN ANCIENT ROME TIMELINE

753 BCE

According to legend, the year Rome was founded by Romulus. It was ruled by kings until . . .

509 BCE

. . . Tarquin the Proud, the last king of Rome, was kicked off the throne.

264 BCE

The First Punic War began, fought between Carthage and Rome. The Punic Wars continued until 146 BCE.

247 BCE

Hannibal, the Carthaginian general, was born.

236 BCE

Scipio the Great was born. He defeated Hannibal in the Second Punic War.

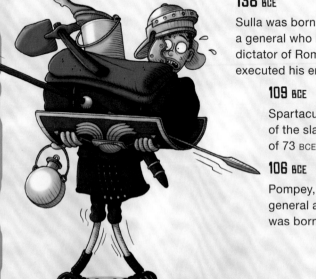

138 BCE

Sulla was born. He was a general who became dictator of Rome and executed his enemies.

109 BCE

Spartacus, the leader of the slave rebellion of 73 BCE, was born.

106 BCE

Pompey, the Roman general and leader, was born.

100 BCE

Julius Caesar was born. He was assassinated by a group of senators in 44 BCE.

83 BCE

Mark Antony was born. He killed himself after the Battle of Actium.

82 BCE

Vercingetorix, the Gallic chieftain who fought Julius Caesar, was born.

63 BCE

Augustus Caesar was born.

32 BCE

The Battle of Actium between Octavian and Cleopatra took place. Afterward, Octavian became Augustus, the "First Citizen" (really the first emperor) of Rome.

10 CE

Around this date, British leader Caractacus was born.

15 OR 16 CE

Agrippina, mother of Emperor Nero, was born.

30 CE

British warrior queen, Boudica, was born around this date.

37 CE

Emperor Nero was born.

43 CE

The Romans invaded Britain under Emperor Claudius.

53 CE

Emperor Trajan was born. He made the Roman Empire the biggest it would ever be.

76 CE

Emperor Hadrian was born.

130 CE

Galen, the famous Roman doctor, was born.

240 CE

Zenobia, warrior queen of Palmyra, was born.

285 CE

Emperor Diocletian divided the Roman Empire in two: the Western Roman Empire and the Eastern Roman Empire.

396 CE

Roman general Flavius Aetius was born.

476 CE

The last emperor of the Western Roman Empire was thrown out by barbarian leader Odoacer. The Eastern Roman Empire continued until 1453, when it was overthrown by the Ottoman Empire.

505 CE

Eastern Roman general, Flavius Belisarius, was born.

LEARNING MORE

BOOKS

Barber, Nicola. *Ancient Romans*. Chicago: World Book, 2009.

Benoit, Peter. *The Ancient World: Ancient Rome*. New York: Scholastic, 2012.

Roberts, Paul. *The Ancient Romans: Their Lives and Their World*. Los Angeles: J. Paul Getty Museum, 2009.

EDUCATIONAL WEBSITES

The Roman Empire, PBS:
www.pbs.org/empires/romans/index.html

Romans, BBC History:
www.bbc.co.uk/schools/primaryhistory/romans

Ten Facts About Ancient Rome, National Geographic Kids:
www.ngkids.co.uk/did-you-know/10-facts-about-the-ancient-Romans

GLOSSARY

ASSASSINS People who commit murder in a surprise attack, usually for political reasons

BARBARIANS People who were considered uncivilized and primitive by the Romans

BESIEGED Surrounded by enemy forces

CENTURION A soldier who is in charge of a century, or a group of 80 legionaries, in the Roman army

COHORTS Groups of soldiers in the Roman army; six centuries (groups of 80 legionaries) make up a cohort

CONSUL The highest ruler of ancient Rome, chosen from the senate

CRUCIFIED Killed by being nailed or tied to a cross and left to die

ELECTED Chosen to be leader

EMPIRE A group of states or countries ruled by one leader or state

EXILE Being banned from your home country

GLADIATOR An armed person who fought with others (often to the death) to entertain a public audience

HOSTAGES People who are held by someone who demands that certain things are done before they are freed

LEGION A group of 5,120 soldiers in the Roman army, consisting of nine cohorts and one prima cohors

LEGIONARY A foot soldier in the Roman army

MARAUDING In search of things to steal or people to attack

OUTLAWED Banned

PARDONED Forgiven or excused

PRIMA COHORS A group of soldiers in the Roman army; 10 centuries (groups of 80 legionaries) make up a prima cohors

PROSCRIPTION The act of banning or condemning

REPUBLIC A country ruled without a king or queen

REVOLT A rebellion

SENATE A group of 300 people called senators who acted as advisers to the leaders of Rome

SENATOR One of 300 members of the senate

TREASON Betraying one's country by going to war against it or helping its enemies

TRIUMVIRATE A group of three people holding power together

INDEX

Aetius, Flavius 32–33, 61
Africa 5, 11, 26–27, 30, 39, 42, 54
Agrippina 24, 34–35, 59
Antony, Mark 14, 38–39, 59
Arabia Petraea 48
Arverni 22–23
assassinate 14, 24, 33, 35, 52, 59
Atrebates 46
Aurelian, Emperor 52–53
Aurelius, Emperor Marcus 50–51
auxiliary soldiers 11

Barbarians 15, 21, 29, 32–33, 54, 56–57
Barca, Hamilcar 8
Battle of Actium 14, 39, 59
Battle of Pharsalus 38, 43
Battle of Silvia Arsia 41
Battle of Zama 29
Belisarius, Flavius 54–55, 61
besieged 23
Boudica 16–17, 60
Britain 16–17, 46–47, 56–57, 59, 60
Brutus 14, 38
Byzantine Empire 29, 54–55

Caesar, Augustus (Octavian) 14–15, 29, 34, 35, 38–39, 59
Caesar, Julius 12–13, 14, 20, 22–23, 29, 38–39, 42–43, 47, 48, 59
Caligula, Emperor 34
Caractacus 46–47, 59
Carthage 8–9, 21, 26–27
Cassius 14, 38
Catuvellauni 46
centurion 11
chariots 16, 24, 40, 49
Christianity 37
civil war 30–31
Claudius, Emperor 20, 34–35, 36, 46–47, 60
Cleopatra 39, 59
Colosseum 49
conquer 8–9, 12–15, 21, 27, 29, 37, 40, 42, 48–49, 52–53, 56
Constantinople 54–55
consuls 12–13, 26, 28, 41
Crassus 13, 19, 31, 42–43
Crixus 19
crucified 19

Dacia 48
dictators 13, 31, 40, 42, 58
doctor 50–51

Eastern Roman Empire 29, 54–55, 60, 61
Egypt 15, 43, 52
elected 12, 15, 28
elephants 9, 27
ethnic groups 9, 16–17, 21, 22, 29, 32–33, 46–47, 56–57

Festivals 37, 49
fire 25
fort 21
Franks 32
Fulvia 39

Galen 50–51, 60
Gaul 13, 22, 32–33
Germany 15, 48
gladiators 18, 49, 50
gods 21, 36–37

Hadrian, Emperor 20–21, 29, 36, 56–57, 60
Hadrian's Wall 21, 37
Hannibal 8–9, 26–27, 58
Huns 32–33

Iceni 16–17
invade 9, 12, 20, 26, 60

Javelin 11, 17
Jews 57
Jugurtha, King 30
Justinian I, Emperor 55

Legionaries 10–11
legions 10–11, 30
Lepidus (cousin of Agrippina) 34
Lepidus, Marcus Aemilius 14, 38–39

Marius 30–31, 42
Mesopotamia 48–49, 56
Mithridates, King 30, 43

Nero, Emperor 24–25, 35, 59, 60
Numidia 30

Octavian see Caesar, Augustus
Odoacer 29, 61
Ostrogoths 54–55

Palmyrenes 52–53, 60
Parthia 49
pirates 42

Pius, Antoninus 57
plague 51
Plot of the Three Daggers 34
poisoned 9, 17, 24, 34, 35
Pompey the Great 13, 31, 38, 42–43, 59
Pontus 30, 43
proscriptions 31
Ptolemy 43
Punic Wars 8, 26, 27, 58

Rebellion 18–19, 42, 48, 55
religion 36–37, 46
republic 15, 28, 29, 41
revolt 16, 57
Roman army 9, 10–11, 14–19, 21, 22–23, 26–27, 30, 32–33, 46–49, 53, 56
Roman Empire 8, 13, 15, 20–21, 28–29, 49, 51, 52, 54–57, 60
Romulus and Remus 28, 40, 58

Sacrifices 37
Sassanids 52–53
Scipio 26–27, 58
senate 12–13, 39, 40
senators 12–13, 38, 40–41, 59
Silures 47
slavery 18–19, 49, 57, 59
Spain 8–9, 12, 15, 26, 39, 42, 48
Spartacus 18–19, 42, 59
stabbed 13, 29, 38
Suetonius 16–17
Sulla 30–31, 42, 58
Syria 27, 43, 52

Tarquin the Proud 28, 40–41, 58
Thrace 18
Trajan, Emperor 20, 48–49, 56, 60
triumph (parade) 42
triumvirate (three-person alliance) 38, 43
Tullia 40
Tullius, Servius 40

Valentinian III 33
Vandals 54
Vercingetorix 22–23, 59
Verica, King 46
Visigoths 32–33

Western Roman Empire 29, 33, 60, 61
wolf 28, 40

Zenobia 52–53, 60